R AMAZING! ™

We find the amazing in the ordinary everyday with lists, polls and quizzes. Helping us to appreciate, in fun and quirky ways, the world in which we live.

Creating interactive content, R Amazing! is a safe place to explore different topics and share your views.

It is ok to disagree with us regarding who or what we think is amazing! We share our thoughts on our website and in our books to enable debate and discussion.

We encourage the expression of opinions in an appropriate way with an understanding that it is ok for people to have differing views.

R Amazing! debates should be conducted politely and respectfully, ending with an agreement and common ground, even if that is to agree to disagree.

www.r-amazing.com

Dogs R Amazing!
Markus Baker & Adam Galvin

Published by R-and-Q.com.
Copyright © 2019 Mark 'Markus' Baker and R-and-Q.com

All rights reserved.
ISBN: 978-1-9161450-6-1

DOGS

R AMAZING! ™

www.r-amazing.com/dogs/

Adam Galvin and Markus Baker
Creators of R Amazing!

"The world would be a nicer place if everyone had the ability to love as unconditionally as a dog."

M.K. Clinton

"

*The only creatures
that are evolved to...*

*...convey pure love
are dogs and infants.*
Johnny Depp

Sniffer Dogs

A sniffer dog is trained to identify things like illegal drugs, electronic devices, blood, currency and explosives. They can sense between 30,000 to 100,000 different smells. Isn't that amazing?

An attempt to smuggle drugs through customs by covering them with a balloon smeared with coffee, petroleum jelly and pepper was foiled by a sniffer dog's fantastic sense of smell.

A dog's nose can even detect human bodily changes caused by fluctuating hormones and even predict pregnancy. In addition to this, they can also sense blood sugar shifts in diabetics and notify the owner by either nudging, barking, sitting or lying down.

> *A blind dog can still smell love.*
> Unknown

Search & Rescue Dogs

Search and Rescue Dogs are assigned to locate missing people in disastrous situations like explosions, earthquakes, fire and snowstorms. St Bernard, which is a breed known for finding people in snow, exhibits high stamina, intelligence, training and scenting ability.

Scenting dogs pick up air particles, whereas trailing dogs smell the ground to detect a scent and tracking dogs follow a path and signs to find a missing person. These adorable heroes risk their lives to save ours.

A dog will teach you unconditional love. If you can have that in your life, things won't be too bad.

Robert Wagner

DID YOU KNOW?

Dogs whisker's help them explore their surroundings by sending information to the brain about the size, shape and speed of any objects in their environment.

Source: https://www.purina.co.uk/dogs/behaviour-and-training/understanding-dog-behaviours/why-do-dogs-have-whiskers

Ever consider what our dogs must think of us? I mean, here we come back from a grocery store with the most amazing haul, chicken, pork, half a cow. They must think we're the greatest hunters on earth!

Anne Tyler

Herding Dogs

During training, a stock dog's natural instinct to prey on animals is honed to give the dog the new skill of herding. The dogs use a variety of techniques. Staying ahead, fetching dogs keep the livestock in a group while the driving dogs direct from the back to push the animals forward.

Stock dogs herd sheep, cattle, ducks and geese. They have even been known to sheppard children into corners to protect them from harm.

> *Sheep, wolves, and sheepdogs – The sheep go through life refusing to see evil. The wolves are the evil preying on the sheep. But the sheepdogs? They protect the sheep. They fight the evil.*
>
> American Sniper Movie

LEARN MORE AT

Hearing Assist Dogs

Clever dogs are trained to transform the lives of people with hearing difficulties. Hearing Assist Dogs alert their companions to the sound of a phone ring, alarm clock, doorbell, fire alarm, cries and more.

Hearing dogs give independence to their owners by becoming their ears. How amazing that a dog can share their ability to hear with their owner.

"My dog can't hear me yelling at him to stop chasing squirrels, but he can hear a cheese wrapper opening from miles away.
SnarkECards

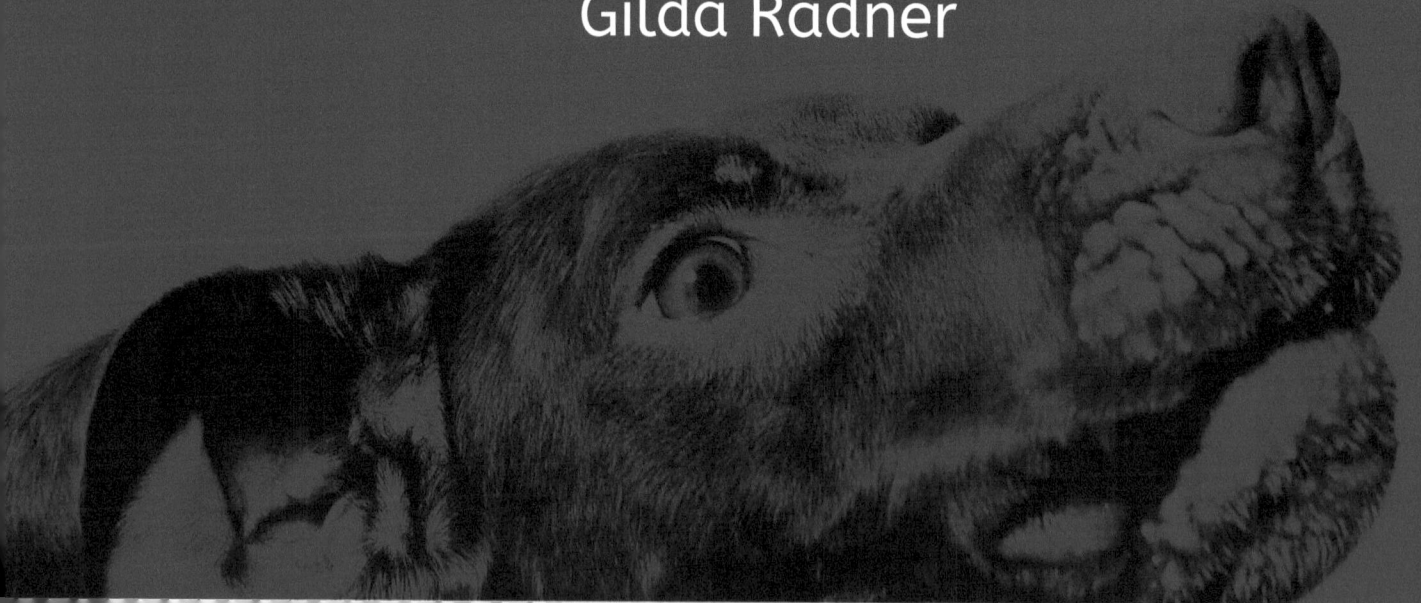

I think dogs are the most amazing creatures; they give unconditional love. For me, they are the role model for being alive.
Gilda Radner

DID YOU KNOW?

At the end of the song 'A Day in the Life'. The Beatles cleverly added a frequency only dogs can hear. So next time you play this song keep an eye out for your dogs' reaction just before this song ends.

Source: https://www.gigwise.com/news/85705/paul-mccartney-reveals-secret-sound-for-dogs-hidden-on-sgt-pepper-album

Dogs are Smart

Border collies, Poodles, and German shepherds are in the top 20% of the most intelligent dog breeds. They can recognise up to 250 words which is more than the 165 that an average 2 and a half-year-old child knows.

Dogs are said to be great problem solvers and can complete basic shape puzzles. Dogs can even do simple addition and know that 1+1=2. They even show surprise when an incorrect answer is revealed.

If you think dogs can't count, try putting three dog biscuits in your pocket and then give him only two of them.

Phil Pastoret

Helping the Blind

When humans can not see, they often need the help of a trained dog, known as a guide dog. But how do guide dogs help people who have limited vision?

They are trained to walk in the centre of the pavement, avoid obstacles, navigate everyday situations and alert their owner to any dangers.

What other tasks do you feel a guide dog could help with?

> *Dogs have given us their absolute all.*
> *We are the center of their universe.*
> *We are the focus of their love and*
> *faith and trust.*
> Roger Caras

DID YOU KNOW?

The very rare occasions that dogs sweat, they do so through their paws. Imagine only being able to sweat through your feet. What a smell!

Source: https://www.livescience.com/55553-do-dogs-sweat.html

No matter how little money and how few possessions you own, having a dog makes you feel rich.

Louis Sabin

Canine Cancer Detection

Humans mainly experience the world with their eyes, while dogs sense it with their nose. Having a 1000 to 10,000 times better-smelling sense than humans, dogs can smell things we cannot, like Cancer.

Dr Claire Guest was inspired to co-found Medical Detection Dogs after her dog began nudging her chest and exhibiting behavioural change. This lead Caire to visit her doctor, discovering and ultimately recovering from her Cancer diagnosis.

" *A dog is the only thing on earth that loves you more than he loves himself.* "

Josh Billings

Ride on Trains

There are around 35,000 stray dogs in Moscow. To make their way around the large city, these street-wise dogs have learnt how to board, ride and depart the subway.

Learning to survive among humans, they have even been known to obey traffic signals and deal with the loud city noises and huge crowds that may frighten other dogs.

These street dogs have become self-sufficient at travelling around the city, finding food and meeting their needs.

There's a world of difference between a dog that is off the leash and a dog that is trained to be off the leash.

Don Sullivan

A well trained dog will make no attempt to share your lunch. He will just make you feel so guilty that you cannot enjoy it.

Helen Thomson

DID YOU KNOW?

Before the 1966 World Cup in England. The trophy was stolen. It was found by Pickles, a mixed breed Collie whilst out for a walk with his owner.

Source: https://en.wikipedia.org/wiki/Pickles_(dog)

Therapy Dogs

Affectionate dogs bring warm smiles and help us heal with their soulful eyes, licking and tail-wagging gestures. Trained dogs serve as emotional support in stressful situations. Humans and dogs share a special bond.

It is hard to ignore a canine friend when it approaches happily wagging its tail. How wonderful to have a friend that never judges you and loves you unconditionally. Therapy dogs can be our best friend.

Could you imagine a dog ever helping you to forget your worries?

> *There is no psychiatrist in the world like a puppy licking your face.*
> Bernard Williams

LEARN MORE AT

www.r-amazing.com/seizure-dogs/

Seizure Assist Dogs

65 million people around the world are reported to have epilepsy.

Seizure Assist Dogs provide an improved quality of life by alerting their owner up to an hour before an oncoming seizure. They help prevent serious injuries by giving their owner time to take any necessary precautions.

Close eye contact, going for help, fetching medication and turning the lights on are the alert indications Seizure Assist Dogs can use to help their owner.

No animal I know of can consistently be more of a friend and companion than a dog.
Stanley Leinwoll

DID YOU KNOW?

In a long-distance race between a Greyhound dog and a Cheetah. The Greyhound would easily win because it can run at 35mph for up to an incredible 7 miles. The Cheetah can run fast for around 250 meters.

Source: https://www.psychologytoday.com/gb/blog/canine-corner/200908/could-dogs-be-the-fastest-land-animals-in-the-world

Once you have had a wonderful dog, a life without one, is a life diminished.

Dean Koontz

Pointing at Objects

Unlike many other animals, who look at the pointing finger, Dogs are clever enough to realise that the gesture is to look at something else further way.

Dogs understand pointing gestures better than Chimpanzees. Your dog becomes alert when you point at something.

Instead of using a finger, dogs tend to use their nose to reciprocate the pointing gesture to alert their owner.

Dogs do speak, but only to those who know how to listen.

Orhan Pamuk

"

Dogs' lives are too short.
Their only fault, really.

Agnes Sligh Turnbull

DID YOU KNOW?

When sleeping and cold, a dog will instinctively curl into a ball to keep themselves warm to protect their vital organs.

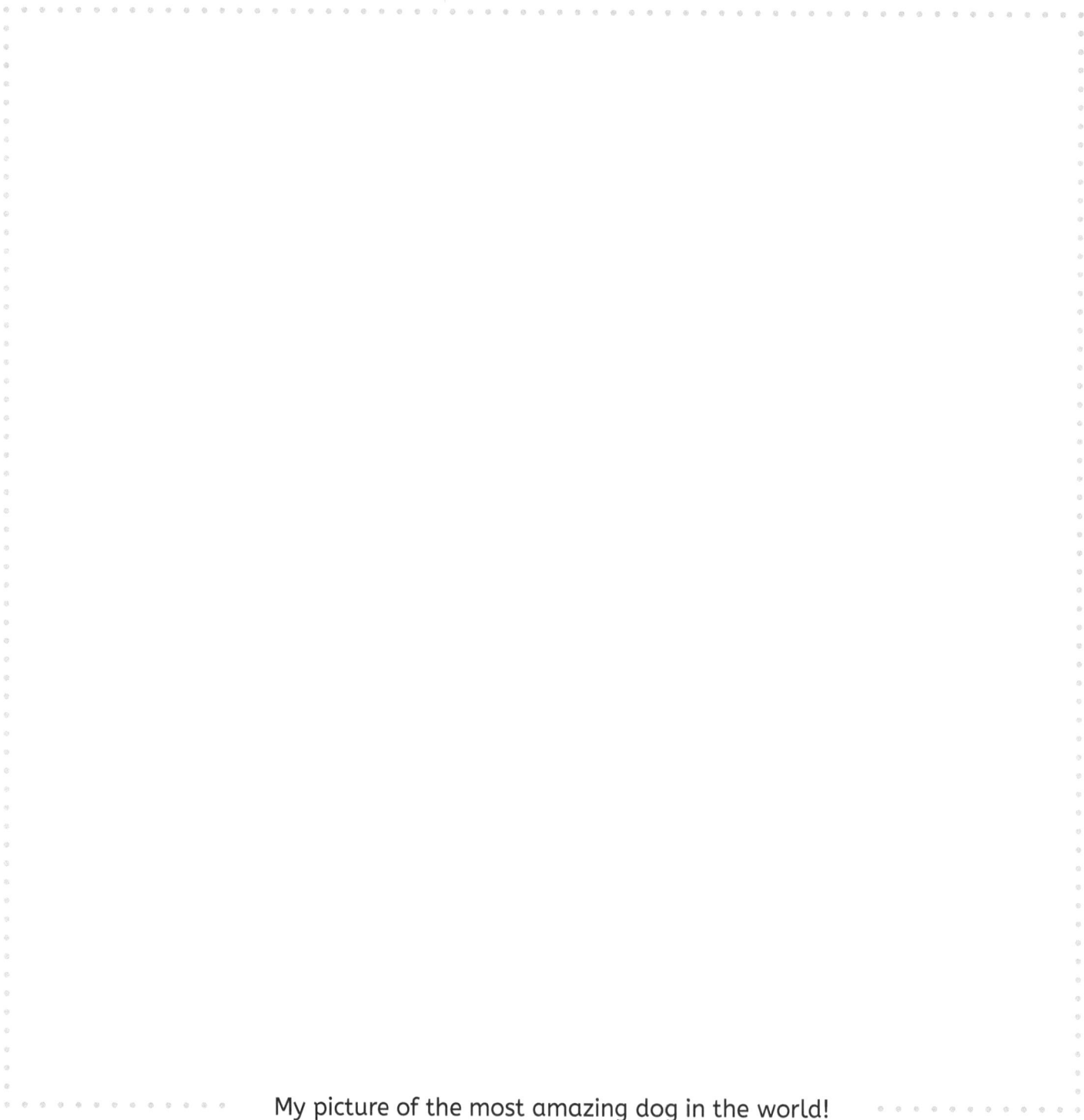

My picture of the most amazing dog in the world!

The most amazing dog in the world is

. . . .

I love it when this amazing dog...

....

....

....

....

....

....

"

This dog is amazing because...

....

....

....

....

"

MORE BOOKS BY R&Q

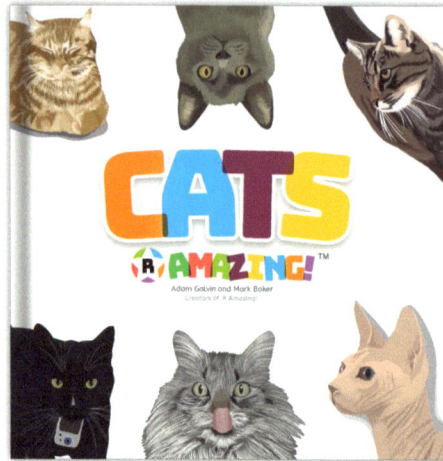

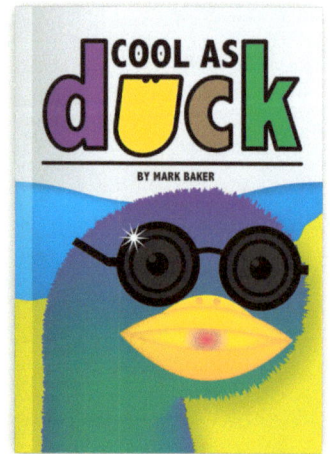

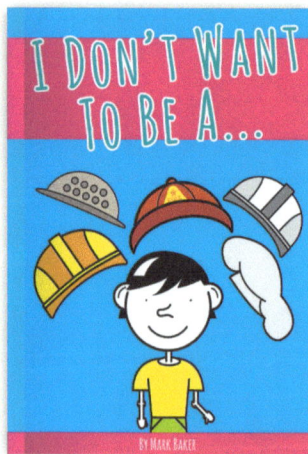

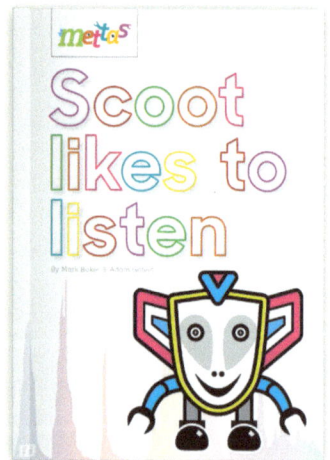

DOOR KNOB FOR A NOSE
BY MARK BAKER & JENNIFER BARSH

CATS R AMAZING!
Adam Galvin and Mark Baker
Creators of R Amazing!

COOL AS dUCK
BY MARK BAKER

I DON'T WANT TO BE A...
By Mark Baker

THIS BOOK NEVER ENDS...
...it keeps looping round and round until somebody says "PLEASE STOP READING NOW!"
Who is going to give up first? The grown up or the child because...
By Mark Baker

mettas
Scoot likes to listen
By Mark Baker